LET MY PEOPLE LAUGH

Let My People Laugh

Published in Nashville, Tennessee, by Thomas Nelson®.
Thomas Nelson® is a registered trademark of Thomas Nelson, Inc.

Thomas Nelson, Inc. titles may be purchased in bulk for educational, business, fund-raising, or sales promotional use. For information, please e-mail SpecialMarkets@ThomasNelson.com.

Project Manager: Lisa Stilwell
Designed by: Thinkpen Design, Inc.
www.thinkpendesign.com

ISBN-10: 1-4041-8694-8
ISBN-13: 978-1-4041-8694-1

Printed in the United States of America

www.thomasnelson.com

09 10 11 12 [RRD] 6 5 4 3 2 1

HOLY HUMOR FOR THE SOUL

LET MY PEOPLE LAUGH

Drew Dyck, Editor

THOMAS NELSON
Since 1798

NASHVILLE   DALLAS   MEXICO CITY   RIO DE JANEIRO   BEIJING

Introduction

Despite what outsiders sometimes assume, church is funny. I grew up in it, so I know.

Some of the memories still make me chuckle. I recall my youth pastor, a man prone to verbal gaffes. His first prayer in front of a congregation wasn't exactly smooth.

"Dear Lod," he started, before clearing his throat to try again. "I mean, Dear Gord."

I also remember a hapless visitor to our congregation, apparently unfamiliar with rhetorical questions. When the pastor paused his sermon to ask, "What would Jesus say to you today?" this man offered his response aloud. "I dunno. Probably 'quit drinking and get a job.'"

Then there's the story of the disruptive child who was hauled out of service by his father for discipline, but not before letting the congregants hear his desperate plea: "Pray for me!"

Life certainly comes with more than its share of stress and heartache. Sometimes the alternative to laughing is crying—or to explode! Pastor Chuck Swindoll writes "humor is not a sin. It is a God-given escape hatch. . .a safety valve." When the pressures of life and ministry mount, a safety valve is exactly what we need.

That's the inspiration behind this book. The tidbits of levity in the following pages are designed to lift your spirit and give it a good shake. The stories and cartoons come from Christianity Today International publications, such as **Leadership** journal, PreachingToday.com, and the Church Laughs e-newsletter. If this book makes you laugh, you can find more material like this at ChristianityToday.com and BuildingChurchLeaders.com.

Before you turn the page, allow me to thank some people who were crucial to making this book happen.

I'd like to acknowledge Mary Keeley, the skilled administrator of ChristianityTodayInternational'sLeadershipTeamandprojectcoordinator Kelli Trujillo for ensuring this book was well organized and completed in a timely manner. Thanks! It wouldn't have happened without you.

I also want to thank Rachel Willoughby, for her tireless work hunting down reams of cartoons—and then for forgiving me when, at the end of the project, I joked that she had accidentally saved the wrong ones and must start over from scratch.

Some believe that ministry is a somber affair, that humor has no place in the church. I disagree. In fact I find the very idea of church a bit amusing. There's a muted hilarity to the whole enterprise—us, a flawed and fumbling band of dreamers trying to function as the body of Christ on earth. I'm sure God smiles. I hope you do too.

—Drew Dyck

Carol Stream, Illinois

Minister Discovers Cure for Gossiping

A minister had two gossipy sisters in his church. One day they saw his car parked in front of the liquor store and began spreading word of their minister's "drinking problem."

When he learned who was spreading the rumor, he parked his car in front of the sisters' house and left it there overnight.

Usher Faux Pas

An elderly woman walked into the local country church. A friendly usher greeted her at the door and helped her up the flight of steps.

"Where would you like to sit?" he asked.

"The front row, please," she answered.

"You really don't want to do that," the usher said. "The pastor is really boring."

"Do you happen to know who I am?" asked the woman.

"No," said the usher.

"I'm the pastor's mother," she replied indignantly.

"Do you know who I am?" the usher asked.

"No," she said.

"Good."

"Come in, Mr. Fenster. Tell me about your problems."

Original Sin

I had just finished a lesson on Christian behavior.
"Now, Billy," I asked, "tell me what we must do
before we can expect to be forgiven for our sins."
Without hesitation, Billy replied, "First we gotta sin."

—Clara Null

Oklahoma City, Oklahoma

"Mr. Norlander, as your gift assessment consultant, I have the task of connecting you with the ministry you have tested most gifted to perform. After much deliberation, it is my conviction that you'd serve the church best as a pew sitter."

"Great message on patience, Pastor.
I loved the way you illustrated by telling
those kids to sit down and shut up."

Going Out with a Bang!

When my dad, a World War II vet, died, he had a military burial with a color guard, taps, and a twenty-one gun salute. A few days later, I learned from our babysitter how my four-year-old daughter, Grace, had described the scene: "I went to a funeral. We went to a church, then we went to the seminary [cemetery], and everyone cried and cried. And then they shot Grandpa, and it was over."

—Mary Officer

West Des Moines, Iowa

"Gesundheit."

"And this petition requests changing the term *sinner* to 'person who is morally challenged.'"

"Is the coast clear?"

"It's a tricky theological point.
You say you covet your neighbor's humility?"

In one simple illustration, Pastor Ken wipes out the
myths of Santa Claus and the Easter Bunny.

Divine Directive

Our three-year-old daughter, Abby, was having trouble sleeping through the night. She kept waking up because she was afraid. Each time I tucked her into bed again, I would remind her that Jesus was with her and that He would keep her safe.

The sleepless nights continued, with Abby seeking comfort in our bedroom. Finally, one night, I asked her if she had prayed for Jesus to take her fear away and help her fall asleep.

"Oh yes," she assured me. "He told me to come and get you!"

—Karen Fair
BUTLER, PENNSYLVANIA

Like Father, Like Son

When my oldest son was six, he was sitting in our church service with his mother while I preached from the pulpit. My topic was parenting, and I was trying to make the point that we must not only talk God's truth, but walk it as well.

I told the congregation that my favorite child-rearing proverb is, "It doesn't matter what you say to your children; they will grow up to be just like you."

After I made that statement, I confessed that it scared me. I then asked if it scared anyone else. I looked out over the congregation to see that the only person with his hand raised was my son.

—Rev. Ronald B. Hughes

Norwood, Ontario

" . . . and our Men's Quiche Fellowship meets
every Sunday morning at seven."

©1986 Bion Smith

"It looks like an offering we can't refuse."

Why Fathers Have Gray Hair

A father passed by his son's bedroom and was astonished to see the bed nicely made up and everything neat and tidy. Then he saw an envelope propped up against the pillow. It was addressed "Dad." Having the worst premonition and with trembling hands, he tore open the envelope and read the letter:

Dear Dad,

It is with great regret and sorrow that I'm writing you. I had to elope with my new girlfriend because I wanted to avoid a scene with you and Mom. I've been finding real passion with Joan, and she is so nice. I knew you would not approve of her because of all her piercings, tattoos, tight motorcycle clothes, and the fact that she is so much older than I am. It's not just her passion, Dad. She really gets me.

Joan says that we are going to be very happy. She owns a trailer in the woods and has a stack of firewood—just enough for the whole winter. We share a dream of having many children.

Please don't worry, Dad. I'm fifteen, and I know how to take care of myself. I'm sure we'll be back to visit someday so you can get to know your grandchildren.

Your son,
Chad

P.S. Dad, none of the above is true. I'm over at Tommy's house. I just wanted to remind you that there are worse things in life than the report card that's in my desk drawer. I love you! Call when it's safe for me to come home.

"According to my horoscope, this is a good week to preach against false doctrines."

"The difficult question was, how badly
did we need this new building?"

Little Girl's Cheerful Offering

A mother gave her child a one-dollar bill and
a quarter.

"Sweetheart," the mother said, "you can place
either one in the offering plate. It's entirely up
to you."

As they were driving home, the mother asked her
daughter what she had decided to give.

"Well, at first I was going to give the dollar," said
the daughter. "But the man behind the pulpit said
God loves a cheerful giver, and I felt I would be
much more cheerful if I gave the quarter instead."

"Our congregation is so small that when the minister says 'dearly beloved,' I get embarrassed."

Unwelcome Confession

Three preachers were on a nonproductive fishing trip when they began to discuss various topics to pass the time. One preacher said he thought it would be nice if they confessed their biggest sins to one another and then prayed for one another. They all agreed, and the first preacher said that his biggest sin was that he liked to sit at the beach now and then and watch pretty women stroll by.

The second preacher confessed that his biggest sin was that he went to the track every so often and put a small bet on a horse.

Turning to the third preacher, they asked, "Brother, what is your biggest sin?"

With a grin, he said, "My biggest sin is gossiping."

"I can't stand to listen to anyone else preach.
You reckon that means the Lord is calling
me to the ministry?"

"And, Father, I ask thee now for a good text to accompany this fantastic joke."

"This song isn't really special to me, but it does provide a wonderful showcase for my voice."

"Look on the bright side—at least you've solved the parking problem."

"This is the pastor's first baptism."

The celebrated roller-ushers of Third Church.

"A man from 'Ripley's Believe It or Not!' wants a picture of someone on fire for the Lord."

When We Fail to Communicate

Old Fred's hospital bed is surrounded by well-wishers, but it doesn't look good. Suddenly, he motions frantically to the pastor for something to write on. The pastor lovingly hands him a pen and a piece of paper. Fred uses his last bit of energy to scribble a note, and then he dies.

The pastor thinks it best not to look at the note right away, so he places it in his jacket pocket. At Fred's funeral, as the pastor is finishing his eulogy, he realizes he's wearing the jacket he was wearing when Fred died.

"Fred handed me a note just before he died," he says. "I haven't looked at it, but knowing Fred, I'm sure there's a word of inspiration in it for us all."

Opening the note, he reads aloud, "Help! You're standing on my oxygen hose!"

The Biggest Liar

A clergyman was walking down the street when he came to a group of about a dozen boys between ten and twelve years of age. The boys surrounded an old dog. Concerned that the boys were hurting the animal, the minister went over and asked, "What are you doing with that dog?"

One of the boys replied, "This dog is just an old stray. We all want him, but only one of us can take him home. So we've decided whichever one of us can tell the biggest lie gets to keep the dog."

The minister was taken aback. "You boys shouldn't have a contest telling lies," he said. "Don't you boys know it's a sin to lie?" Then he launched into a ten-minute sermon about lying. The clergyman ended his speech with "When I was your age, I never told a lie."

There was dead silence for about a minute, and just as the minister was beginning to think he'd gotten through to them, the smallest boy gave a deep sigh and said, "All right. Give him the dog."

As heard from Joel Osteen, — Gino Grunberg
GIG HARBOR, WASHINGTON

"You're in a rut, Reverend.
Every time I come here,
you preach about the Resurrection."

"I know it's early, Pastor,
but I figured you'd be up praying."

"They're either very solid or going nowhere."

"My wife just left me, I lost my job, I need surgery, and my spirits have hit bottom? Pastor, you've gotta help me. What's the difference between pre-, post-, and amillennialism?"

Island Church Hopper

A man was stranded on the proverbial desert island in the Pacific for years. One day when a boat came sailing into view, the man frantically waved and got the skipper's attention. The boat landed on the beach, and the skipper got out to greet the stranded man.

After a while, the rescuing sailor asked the castaway, "What are those three huts you've built?"

The stranded man replied, "That first hut is my house."

"What's that next hut?" asked the sailor.

"I built that for my church."

"What about the third hut?"

"Oh," the castaway answered solemnly, "that's where I used to go to church."

—J. Richard Love

RUSTON, LOUISIANA

"This is my fourth sermon on the transforming power of the gospel. Why do you look like the same old bunch?"

"Yes. Yes. I see that hand."

Swearing Off Swearing

A little boy was sitting sadly on the curb beside his lawn mower, when along came a minister riding a bicycle. The minister noticed that the boy appeared discouraged, so he thought he would try to help.

"Hello there!" said the minister. "How would you like to trade your lawn mower for this bicycle?"

"Sure, mister," the little boy responded, and he went on his merry way.

A few days later, the boy and the minister crossed paths again. The minister said, "I think you took me on our trade. I keep crankin' that old lawn mower, but it won't start."

"You gotta cuss at it," said the little boy.

"I can't do that," said the minister. "I'm a preacher. I forgot about cussin' a long time ago."

The little boy answered, "Just keep on crankin', preacher. It'll come back to ya."

—Van Morris

Mount Washington, Kentucky

"We don't know what you're doing in here, but we've been waiting five minutes to talk to you about the broken hand dryer in the ladies' room."

"The church library just hasn't turned out the way we had hoped."

Too Much to Swallow

A certain pastor observed a little girl standing outside the Sunday school classroom, waiting for her parents to pick her up for "big church." The pastor noticed that she clutched a storybook under her arm with the title **Jonah and the Whale.**

Feeling mischievous, he knelt beside the girl and asked, "What's that you have in your hand?"

"This is my storybook about Jonah and the whale," she answered.

"Tell me something," he continued. "Do you believe that story about Jonah and the whale?"

The girl said, "Of course I believe it!"

The pastor inquired further. "You really believe a man can be swallowed up by a big whale, stay inside him all that time, and come out okay?"

She declared, "Yes! This story is in the Bible, and we talked about it in Sunday school today."

Then the pastor asked, "Can you prove to me this story is true?"

She thought for a moment and then said, "Well, when I get to heaven, I'll ask Jonah."

Finally the pastor asked, "What if Jonah's not in heaven?"

The girl put her hands on her hips and sternly declared, "Then you can ask him!"

—Rich Tatum

CAROL STREAM, ILLINOIS

Story Time

A pastor loved telling stories to the children in his congregation. He'd call the children up to the front of the church, they'd sit on the floor, and he'd tell them a story. One day he said, "Boys and girls, I want to tell you a story about someone who likes to live in the woods, but sometimes we can see him in our own yard. Anybody have any idea who I am talking about?"

No takers. He said, "I want to tell you about a creature that lives in the woods and sometimes in our yards, has a big bushy tail, and likes to eat nuts. Anybody have any idea what I'm talking about?"

No takers. He said, "I'm talking about a creature that lives in the woods, sometimes visits our yard, has a big bushy tail, eats nuts, likes to climb trees, and jumps from tree to tree. Now does anybody know what I'm talking about?"

Wanting to take the pastor out of his misery, a boy raised his hand. The pastor said, "Do you know what I'm thinking about?"

"Well, I know the answer should be Jesus, but it sounds like a squirrel to me."

BASED ON HADDON ROBINSON IN PREACHINGTODAY.COM

"I'll preach on Thanksgiving, Christmas, New Year's, and Easter. You can have 'The Role of Women in the Church,' 'Tongues Speaking for Today,' 'Biblical Inerrancy,' and our special 'Fund Drive Sunday.'"

"I've stopped expecting you to make leaps of faith, but it would be nice to see a hop now and then."

Bulletin Bloopers

So, you're sitting in church, scanning the bulletin, and you read this: "Don't let worry kill you—. Let the church help."

Oops! Yes, that line actually appeared in a real church bulletin. Here are some other notable bulletin bloopers:

"The Odor of Worship is as follows."

"This afternoon, there will be meetings in the south and north ends of the church. Children will be baptized at both ends."

"Thursday night: Potluck supper. Prayer and medication to follow."

"Remember in prayer the many who are sick of our church and community."

"This being Easter Sunday, we will ask Mrs. Lewis to come forward and lay an egg on the altar."

FROM "STRANGE WORLD," Campus Life

Pastor Greer's attempt to raise his youth group's consciousness of Third World poverty was not entirely successful.

"Welcome, O weary searcher for truth!
Say, have you ever worked with kids?"

Delicate Doctrine

Comedian Emo Philips used to tell this story:

In conversation with a person I had recently met, I asked, "Are you Protestant or Catholic?"

My new acquaintance replied, "Protestant."

I said, "Me too! What franchise?"

He answered, "Baptist."

"Me too!" I said. "Northern Baptist or Southern Baptist?"

"Northern Baptist," he replied.

"Me too!" I shouted.

We continued to go back and forth. Finally I asked, "Northern conservative fundamentalist Baptist, Great Lakes Region, Council of 1879 or Northern conservative fundamentalist Baptist, Great Lakes Region, Council of 1912?"

He replied, "Northern conservative fundamentalist Baptist, Great Lakes Region, Council of 1912."

I said, "Die, heretic!"

FROM THE EDITORS OF Leadership Journal

©1996 Dik LaPine

Vanity

A young woman went to her pastor and said, "Pastor, I have a besetting sin, and I want your help. I come to church on Sunday and can't help thinking I'm the prettiest girl in the congregation. I know I ought not think that, but I can't help it. I want you to help me."

The pastor replied, "Mary, don't worry. In your case, it's not a sin. It's just a horrible mistake."

—Haddon Robinson

IN PREACHINGTODAY.COM

Armed to the teeth, Sunday school teacher
Nat Willowby prepares to do battle
with the forces of darkness.

"As you can see on your handouts, today's topic is original sin."

The whole church watched with nervous anticipation
as the visitors sat where the Martins have sat for 42 years.

A Saint by Comparison

Two brothers had terrorized a small town for decades. They were unfaithful to their wives, abusive to their children, and dishonest in their business. When the younger brother died unexpectedly, the surviving brother went to the pastor of the local church.

"I'd like you to conduct my brother's funeral," he said, "but it's important to me that, during the service, you tell everyone my brother was a saint."

"But he was far from that," the minister countered.

The wealthy brother pulled out his checkbook. "Reverend, I'm prepared to give $100,000 to your church. All I'm asking is that you publicly state that my brother was a saint."

On the day of the funeral, the pastor began his eulogy this way: "Everyone here knows that the deceased was a wicked man, a womanizer, and a drunk. He terrorized his employees and cheated on his taxes."

Then he paused. "But as evil and sinful as this man was, compared to his older brother, he was a saint!"

—Greg Asimakoupoulos
MERCER ISLAND, WASHINGTON

© 1988 Steve Phelps

"I wish he were a little less specific
with his illustrations."

Church Lingo Translated

In a never-ending effort to attract the unchurched, some churches have considered translating their unfamiliar terminology into familiar football phrases. Although these definitions are not the best football and certainly not the best theology, they would help initiate football fans into the complexities of church life.

EXTRA POINT: What you receive when you tell the preacher his sermon was too short

FACE MASK: Smiling and saying everything is fine when it isn't

BLOCKING: Talking endlessly to the pastor at the church door and keeping everyone else from exiting

DRAFT CHOICE: The decision to sit close to an air-conditioning vent

DRAW PLAY: What restless children do during a long sermon

END AROUND: Diaper-changing time in the nursery

END ZONE: The pews

FORWARD MOTION: The invitation at an evangelistic service

FULLBACK: What the choir sees while the sermon is delivered

HALFBACK: What the organist sees

HASH MARKS: Stains left on the tablecloth after a potluck

ILLEGAL USE OF HANDS: Clapping at an inappropriate point in the service

ILLEGAL MOTION: Leaving before the benediction

IN THE POCKET: Where some church members keep God's tithe

INCOMPLETE PASS: A dropped offering plate

INTERFERENCE: Talking during the prelude

LINEBACKER: A statistic used by a preacher to support a point just made

PASSING GAME: The maneuver required of latecomers when the person sitting at the end of the pew won't slide to the middle

QUARTERBACK: What tightwads want after putting fifty cents in the offering

RUNNING BACKS: Those who make repeated trips to the restroom

THROUGH THE UPRIGHTS: Getting things done via the elders or church board

TOUCHBACK: The laying on of hands

TWO-MINUTE WARNING: The chairman of the board looking at his watch in full view of the preacher

—William Ellis
Leadership Journal

"Come along quietly, Carl. Your latest birthday puts you with the Middle Agers."

"I think the deaf interpreter is ad-libbing again."

"Clapping or nonclapping?"

All Souped Up

When a friend asked her four-year-old daughter to fetch a can of soup from the pantry, she replied, "But it's dark and scary in there!"

"You don't have to be afraid," came her mother's calm reply. "Jesus is always with you, even in the pantry."

The girl thought for a moment, walked over to the pantry, stuck her head in the door, and called, "Jesus, if You're in there, can You hand me a can of soup?"

—Andrea Miller

GREENVILLE, SOUTH CAROLINA

Pressing On to Win the Prize

My five-year-old grandnephew was obviously worried as he looked down the long aisle of the church where his aunt was to be married the following day. His grandmother had an idea. "I think I'll give a prize to the person who does the best job tomorrow," she told him.

We were all holding our breath the next day, but when it was time, the ring bearer performed without a hitch.

When his grandmother told him he had won the prize, he was both excited and relieved.

"I was pretty sure I had it," he admitted, "until Aunt Dana came in wearing that white dress, and the horn was blowing. Then I started thinking she might win!"

—Barbara Lee
GOLDSBORO, NORTH CAROLINA

"Some churches use the acronym TULIP to remember their beliefs. We use CHRYSANTHEMUM."

"By the time my outpatient surgery got to the end of the prayer chain, I'd had all my limbs amputated, died, and left $100,000 to the building fund."

© 1992 Rob Portlock

PORTLOCK

"We have a special gift today for a lady who hasn't missed a service in 45 years. Eleanor Smith! Where is Eleanor sitting? Eleanor? Eleanor . . . ."

Just Between You and . . .

While hiding a birthday present for another member of the family, my sister Margie asked her little four-year-old granddaughter, Lindsey, if she could keep a secret. Her eyes got big and she answered, "Oh yes, Grandma! I can! But sometimes the people I tell the secret to can't!"

—Tom Kovach
PARK RAPIDS, MINNESOTA

"Dear Timothy, I'm sending under separate cover extra copies of the spiritual gifts inventory quiz for your church."

"Lord, I lay before You the prayer concerns voiced this morning . . . even though most of 'em sound like whining to me."

Splitting Hairs

I recently had the following exchange with my seven-year-old daughter, Carolyn:

"Daddy, why do you have such hairy arms?"

"I don't know, honey. I guess God just wanted to give me a lot of hair on my arms."

"Well, He sure didn't do much with your forehead."

—William H. Ross

LA CROSSE, WISCONSIN

"About my loaves and fishes . . .
could I get a receipt for tax purposes?"

"Our church's distinctive is to be a church of grace.
If anyone can't adhere to that,
we simply ask the person to leave."

Obey—or Else!

Our six-year-old daughter, Lori, was learning
1 Samuel 15:22—"To obey is better than sacrifice"—
for her Bible memory course. One day as she saw her
three-year-old sister, Kristi, being disobedient, she
immediately applied the verse in her interpretation
of the verse. "Kristi," she admonished sternly, "if
you don't obey, you will be sacrificed!"

—Luella Bredin
PRINCE EDWARD ISLAND, CANADA

Hail to the Leaf?

I was sharing the biblical story of Moses with my three-year-old son, Carson. As I read the children's book to him, we came to the part where God speaks to Moses by means of a burning bush. Carson was wide-eyed in wonder as he asked in almost a whisper, "Mommy, was it George Bush?"

—Leanne Waterworth

OSCEOLA, WISCONSIN

"Cheer up! Most youth pastors don't receive ANY housing allowance."

A Permanent Solution

My wife and I teach first-grade Sunday school, and we sometimes laugh at the things our students say. Once, while teaching a lesson on forgiving others, I asked the following question: "What would you do if your best friend hit you?" Several children said, "Tell on him" or "Hit back."

Anna, looking quite thoughtful, slowly raised her hand. When I called on her, she said firmly, "I'd get a new best friend!"

—Joseph Collier

GAINESVILLE, GEORGIA

Sunday, 9:30 A.M., the elite visitor awareness
commandos go into action.

Peter and Pork

At the beginning of our children's Bible club meetings, we always review the previous week's lesson. One evening, to start the conversation about Peter's vision of the heavenly sheet filled with animals, another teacher asked, "What did Peter see when he went up on the housetop to pray?"

One little boy waved his hand and yelled, "Pigs in a blanket!"

—Karen S. Stanfill
Bolivar, Ohio

"Now, while the instruments play,
please shake hands with two people
who aren't in your clique."

"Looks like someone's been sheep-stealing again."

"And after the services we hope you'll join us for coffee, cappuccino, decaf cappuccino, double-decaf cappuccino, latté, latté mocha, mocha java, double mocha decaf..."

"God calls us to evangelism! The bank that holds our mortgage has mentioned it, too."

"The question is, how do we win the world to Christ . . .
with a minimum of fuss and bother?"

Seekers of the Old Testament

"This is Carlo. He's here to translate my sermon
to the youth of our church."

Changeless Savior

While coloring a picture of Jesus in her Bible coloring book one day, my daughter Amy (then three) said, "Daddy, did you know Jesus never changes?"

I was amazed—and delighted—that my little girl understood that God is the same yesterday, today, and forever.

"You're right, Amy," I replied. "Jesus never changes."

To which she added, intent on her artwork, "Yeah, He always wears long sleeves."

—Gary Turner

MULINO, OREGON

"Well, I haven't actually *died* to sin,
but I did feel kind of faint once."

"It was loud, forceful, and clashed with my sensibilities. And that was just your tie."

Unexpected Vacancy

My friend's granddaughter once directed a group of four-year-olds in their Christmas pageant. Everything moved along smoothly until the children playing Mary and Joseph arrived at the inn in Bethlehem.

"Do you have any room for us?" asked young Joseph.

"No, the inn is full," replied the innkeeper.

"But it's so cold outside, and my wife is going to have a baby," pleaded Joseph. "Don't you have any place for us?"

To the surprise of the director and the audience, instead of showing the couple to the stable, the four-year-old innkeeper replied compassionately, "I'm not supposed to say this, but you come right on in."

—Christy Ehmann
PERKASIE, PENNSYLVANIA

"Okay—we'll do the rock service, but forget about rapping the Nicene Creed."

"I pray that this song I'm about to sing will not only speak to your heart, but that it will spiritually rip you limb from limb and lay you barren, naked, and writhing in conviction on the cold, dank, tile floor . . . Amen, God bless you."

"Oldies Night" at the contemporary church.

Huge Jesus

When our son Michael was young, I would sit on his bed during nighttime prayers. When I prayed, I focused my eyes on a heating/air-conditioning vent in the ceiling, never suspecting this had any effect on Michael.

But one day in the mall, my four-year-old looked up at a fifteen-foot vent and exclaimed, "Oh my goodness. Look at that huge Jesus!" It was definitely time to have a long talk.

—Glenna McKelvie

MONTGOMERY, TEXAS

" . . . so my friend Marge said it might be phlebitis, but when I asked the doctor, he said, 'Don't worry. Just stay off your feet for a couple days,' but I told him, 'Now how do you expect me to . . .' "

©1987 Dan Pegoda

WHEN A HYMN WRITER DAYDREAMS...

"We'll hear Pastor's points one and two, skip three, and conclude with point four."

"Sir, you have been recommended for our remedial singing class that meets in the basement of our annex."

Lost in Translation

My Spanish professor told us about an American youth group that had visited her church in Lima, Peru. Apparently, they didn't know Spanish, so they simply added "o" to the end of English words and hoped they turned out right.

One American girl was being teased by the pastor of the church. Feeling embarrassed, she opted to use embarrassado, not knowing it means "pregnant." So the church was understandably startled when this teen girl got up and said, "I am very embarrassado, and it's all the pastor's fault!"

—Kimberly Rae
Norwalk, Ohio

Noah's Last Name

During a weekend visit with my sister, I read to her granddaughter Adrienna from her children's Bible storybook. After our story time, I quizzed Adrienna on what we read.

"Who was the man with the big boat?"

"Noah," she piped right up.

Then—I don't know why—I asked, "What was his last name?"

"Zark!" she replied with authority.

—Donna M. Cotner
HOPEWELL, VIRGINIA

"Okay, the only fair way to do it this morning is . . . heads it's the hymnal, tails it's choruses."

" . . . and I got that scar from the chairman of the board during the second battle of 'Guitars in the Sanctuary' back in '71."

God Has Left the Building

When my identical twin sons were only three, our pastor and his family were moving to Utah to do missionary work. As I hurried to get my children into the car, one twin, Josh, was straggling behind.

"Come on, honey. We have to get going," I said. "Pastor and his family are leaving today. We have to go say good-bye."

He stopped and looked very sad. "Oh no, Mom. Now who's gonna be God?"

—Kira Knobloch

Allegan, Michigan

© 1987 Lee Johnson

Pastor Linquist can never hear "A Mighty Fortress Is Our God" without remembering his old youth group singing it to the tune of "Come on Baby, Light My Fire."

Spontaneity was the charm that defined Fidgeville Temple's success

"And now, on verse three, all those who are balding join in with those who have a mole on their neck."

Here Comes the Groom

At the spring wedding of an older couple, my parents waited with the rest of the guests for the celebration to begin. The church organist played through her entire repertoire of wedding songs, but nothing happened. Not wanting to repeat herself, she continued with Easter hymns in keeping with the season. Soon the door to the pastor's study opened. A shaky, ashen groom appeared just as the organist completed the first line of "Up from the Grave He Arose."

—Sharon Espeseth

BARRHEAD, ALBERTA

THE ULTIMATE TORTURE FOR THE CHOIR DIRECTOR (AMONG OTHERS)...

SOMETHING HAS BEEN LAID ON MY HEART...

© 1991 Doug Hall

HALL

Atomic alto Gladys Thundermuffin departs from the selection listed in the bulletin to do a solo interpretation of the Hallelujah Chorus.

Freudian Slip

My husband is the pastor at our church, and he often calls on different members to lead the congregation in prayer. One man, having been asked to pray, was nervously trying to thank God for our ability to come together for corporate worship. Instead, getting tongue-tied, he prayed, "Thank You for this time of corporal punishment."

—Angela O'Keefe

RAMER, TENNESSEE

"Believe me, fellows, everyone from the Pharaoh on down is an equally valued member of the team."

"Now, as your treasurer, when I talk about our going into Chapter 11, I'm not talking about the book of Matthew."

"Ever had one of those days when you felt
you just had to rebuke someone?"

It was safe to say that Pastor Mel's
vision statement hadn't yet caught fire.

A Ticket in the Wrong Direction

A drunken man got on the bus late one night, staggered up the aisle, and sat next to a woman who was clutching a Bible.

She looked the wayward drunk up and down and said, "I've got news for you, mister. You're going straight to hell!"

The man jumped up out of his seat and shouted, "Oh man, I'm on the wrong bus again!"

—Keith Todd

IN SERMONFODDER.COM

Give the Prodigal Credit

While putting my four-year-old daughter to bed one evening, I read her the story of the prodigal son. We discussed how the young son had taken his inheritance and left home, living it up until he had no money left. Finally, when he couldn't even eat as well as the pigs were eating, he went home to his father, who welcomed him. When we finished the story, I asked my daughter what she had learned. After thinking a moment, she quipped, "Never leave home without your credit card!"

—Jolene Horn

ATASCADERO, CALIFORNIA

© 1985 Doug Hall

"This year our special Christmas offering will go to cover damages and lawsuits resulting from the donkey running amuck at our living Nativity."

"The Baptism"

©1982 Leadership; Concept: Jim Reapsome Art: Larry

"Whatever we decide about the pastor's salary, let's keep in mind all those sermons last year on the simple lifestyle."

"That was the best sermon on giving I've ever heard."

© 1983 Joe Suggs

"Our TitheVision board seems
to be working out well, Fred."

"It's showtime, baby!"

Families during the Holidays

An elderly man in Phoenix calls his son in New York and says, "I hate to ruin your day, but I have to tell you that your mother and I are divorcing. Forty-five years of misery is enough."

"Pop, what are you talking about?" the son asks.

"We can't stand the sight of each other any longer," the old man says. "We're sick of each other, and I'm sick of talking about this, so you call your sister in Chicago and tell her."

Frantic, the son calls his sister, who explodes on the phone. "Like heck they're getting divorced!" she shouts. "I'll take care of this."

She calls Phoenix immediately and screams at her father, "You are not getting divorced. Don't do a single thing until I get there. I'm calling my brother back, and we'll both be there tomorrow. Until then, don't do a thing."

The old man hangs up the phone and turns to his wife. "Okay," he says. "They're coming for Thanksgiving and paying their own fares. Now what do we do for Christmas?"

Taken from the Internet; —Van Morris
MOUNT WASHINGTON, KENTUCKY

Repentance in Process

The story is told of a shoplifter who writes to a department store and says, "I've just become a Christian, and I can't sleep at night because I feel guilty. So here's $100 that I owe you."

Then he signs his name, and in a little postscript at the bottom he adds, "If I still can't sleep, I'll send you the rest."

—Bill White

Paramount, California

The Purpose of Coffee Hour

Coffee was always served at our church after the service. One Sunday our minister asked one of the smaller members of the congregation if he knew why we had coffee hour.

Without hesitating, the youngster replied, "To wake people up before they have to drive home."

—Richard Blake

San Luis Obispo, California

"With our current hard feelings, would anyone object to my praying with my eyes open?"

With Love from Colorado

The deacons' wives held a dessert one evening to welcome our new pastor's wife. To further acquaint her with Colorado and the church, the secretaries hurriedly typed questions to be randomly selected and answered by the deacons' wives. One question stole the show with its typographical error: "Why do you like loving in Colorado?" Naturally, the shiest wife got the question. She read it out loud, blushed, then stammered, "I guess . . . uh . . . because of the cold nights."

—Joan Arpin

LAKEWOOD, COLORADO

Singing from the Heart

In the middle of the solo at church, my young grandson Chandler tugged on my sleeve and whispered, "She can't sing very well, can she?"

Knowing the woman had a deep love for the Lord, I said, "Chandler, she sings from her heart. That's what makes it good." He nodded thoughtfully.

Several days later as he and I were singing along with the car radio, Chandler stopped and said, "Nana, you sing from your heart, don't you?"

—Barbara McKeever

Urbana, Ohio

"Welcome to the church. Would you care to join a coup against the current pastor?"

Sunday morning's guest speaker
miraculously averts a church split.

"I take it there's something you haven't told me."

Banishment by Baptism

When I was a young preacher, my small church had limited facilities, so we held baptisms in a creek. With alligators in the area, however, that was less than ideal.

Then a minister friend suggested I bring my next group of baptismal candidates to his church for a joint baptismal service. Naturally, I accepted.

The baptismal pool had a clear front so the congregation could see everything. When the baptisms were finished, curtains were drawn, and I was left alone in the pool for a moment. The building had no air conditioning, and it was quite hot. I thought how nice it would feel to take a little dip. I glided to one end, turned, and backstroked to the other end.

Hearing a riotous uproar in the church, I looked toward the congregation. The curtain was down only to the top of the glass! An astonished and amused congregation had been watching my every move.

Although it was probably the best laugh that church ever had, I was never invited back to repeat the performance.

—Doug Woodall

JACKSONVILLE BEACH, FLORIDA

"I'd like to thank the board for this lovely plant
you sent to me after our disagreement."

"In the minutes, should I record this as a 'vigorous theological discussion' or a 'serious ecclesiastical debate'?"

"The Wednesday Bible Study, Saturday Prayer Breakfast, Crib Nursery, and Women's Mission Society have declared their independence and will exist as a commonwealth with details regarding defense to be worked out at a later date."

"We interrupt this sermon to inform you that the 4th grade boys are now in complete control of their Sunday school class and are holding Miss Moseby hostage."

"Pastor, I hate to complain,
but I want to do what I do best."

Needed: More Johns

Before its renovation, our church lacked adequate restroom facilities. One Sunday, Pastor Dennis, preaching about the attributes of John the Baptist, didn't know why the congregation snickered after his emphatic statement: "What this church needs is more Johns."

—Esther L. Vogt
HILLSBORO, KANSAS

First Baby, Fifth Floor

On one of my pastoral visits, I had just stepped inside a hospital elevator and punched the button for the fifth floor when a young pregnant woman slipped in beside me.

Noticing that she glanced at the button panel but didn't press a button for another floor, I asked, "Number five?"

"Heavens no!" she gasped. "It's only my first!"

—Preston A. Taylor

Hondo, Texas

© 1979 Larry Thomas

"Why can't he just read his resignation
like other pastors do?"

"And until next Sunday, remember . . . God loves you, I love you, and Brother Al here is working on it."

After a very brief discussion, the board of trustees
dismissed Herb's charge that the church
had become infatuated with youth.

Armed and Nutritious

My two daughters, Arian and Andrea, and I were leaving with a casserole for a church potluck on the other side of town. Because our route would take us through some rough neighborhoods, my husband, Rick, expressed concern.

I'm not sure his fears were completely allayed when fourteen-year-old Arian said, "Don't worry about us, Dad. We've got broccoli, and we know how to use it."

—Jenna L. Houp
FORT MITCHELL, KENTUCKY

No Stars for You

Our church was without a building, as was another church nearby. We both ended up worshiping in a town building: Our congregation met on the third floor, and the other church met on the second floor.

The arrangement worked fine until one Sunday, when our congregation started singing "Will There Be Any Stars in My Crown?" Just as we finished that line, the second-floor congregation sang out, "No, Not One."

–Mary Jane Kurtz
GREEN ISLAND, NEW YORK

"Next the children will recreate the church split that led to the founding of this church."

"He was traded to Valley Church for a
music director and a youth pastor."

"I don't know why everyone criticizes our committee; we haven't done a thing."

©1989 Steve Phelps

Mistaken Identity

Whenever my six-year-old niece, Katie, was asked her name, her standard response was "I'm Katie, Pastor Allen's daughter." Thinking she needed to assert her own identity, Katie's mother encouraged her to simply reply "Katie."

The next day, a man asked her name. "I'm Katie," she replied.

"Oh, you're Pastor Allen's daughter," he said, smiling.

"Well, Dad says so," said Katie, "but Mom's not real sure."

—Aunt Rene

Grapeland, Texas

Just Shut Up

Several years ago when our new assistant minister was delivering his first sermon to the congregation, an elderly woman in one of the front pews shouted, "Oh, shut up!"

The young preacher, taken aback, stopped midsentence, held on to the pulpit, and, with his mouth agape, stared at the displeased parishioner. He soon discovered that her harsh words had been directed not at him, but at her squeaking hearing aid.

—Eva R. Priestley

Mt. Laurel, New Jersey

©1997 Rick Stromoski

—STRoMoski—

"I'm aware that some of us take our leadership role a bit more seriously than others..."

"Church hoppers."

Wrong Body

Carol, a gracious clerk in our local Christian bookstore, often refers to a church as "the body." One week, many devoted members of a local "body" had come to the bookstore to buy birthday gifts for their pastor. The following week, their Pastor John stopped by the store. He told Carol about the surprise party his congregation had given him the night before. Carol's heart was touched. Spontaneously, she leaned forward and exclaimed, "Oh, John, I just love your 'body'!"

–Martha E. Garrett

East Wenatchee, Washington

"No, I clearly said *Thanks*-giving service."

"Rover, your gift test indicates you'd do best at fetching and sitting at my feet; but our family needs someone to sit on the branches and sing. Do you think you could handle that?

Grin and Bear It

A friend of mine used to teach Sunday school, and her favorite hymn to sing in class was "Oh, the Consecrated Cross I Bear."

One Sunday, a concerned mother questioned my friend about a song her child said she'd learned in class. Her daughter had been singing, "Oh, the constipated, cross-eyed bear!"

—Kirsten Jackson
Durant, Oklahoma

"Oh, thank you, Pastor. Talking to you is almost like being able to talk to Oprah."

"He remained on the same point for so long
he went into screensaver mode."

© 2002 Tim Walburg

© Steve Phelps

"I thought you said, 'cutting EDGE' ministry!"

William functioned best in a small group with others like himself.

That's three verses for and three verses against. . .
in the mood for a little **Apocrypha**?

We're hoping you'll lead us on a journey of transformation without requiring any real changes.

FLETCHER

Are you absolutely sure 'hide and watch' is
not a leadership style?

FLETCHER

Our new pastor is a master at delegating.

Funny Footwork

We had gathered at my pastor's house for our church's monthly leadership meeting. Assembled around the dining room table were the elders, the deacons, and their spouses. My pastor's little dog loved to sit under the table and let us rub our feet on her back and belly. I had my shoes off and felt her bump me, so I happily rubbed my feet on her while the pastor talked about integrity and accountability.

Suddenly, I heard a bark, and there was the dog—across the room. I threw up the tablecloth to find I had been playing footsies with an elder. "I thought it was the dog!" I blurted out as my face turned a million shades of red.

"I sure wondered," said the equally embarrassed man.

—Diana Mylek
Waterville, Ohio

Mass Marriage

My husband, a pastor, is often asked to officiate at weddings. During a well-booked wedding season, we were preparing for one son's birthday party. When I asked him whom he wanted to invite, the only names he gave were his "girl friends."

Which one are you going to marry when you grow up?" I asked jokingly.

Without hesitation he replied, "When I grow up, I'm going to be a pastor and marry them all."

—Marian Obeda
LONDON, ONTARIO

Frankly, I find certain elements of biblical imagery a bit disturbing.

It's a new church record...you went from un-churched to churched to over-churched and back to un-churched in less than two years

FLETCHER

Stand By Your Man

My husband and I attended a large church in Southern California. One Sunday, at the close of the service, I found myself trapped in a large group of people moving toward the side exit of the church. Not wanting to get separated from my husband, I grabbed onto his arm. He pulled on my arm teasingly as if he wanted me to let go. I pulled his arm close to me and let him lead me out of the church. As we walked through the door, he again tried to free his arm. Again, I pulled it close to my side and said, "I'm not going to let you go."

"Well, my wife may have something to say about that," said a voice belonging to the arm—but sounding nothing like my husband! I looked up to see I was holding the arm of one of our church elders, while my husband waited in sidesplitting mirth about forty yards ahead.

–Jan Brown
MOORESVILLE, NORTH CAROLINA

On Second Thought

My seven-year-old daughter, Jessica, is a deep thinker when it comes to theological questions. Recently we discussed why bad things sometimes happen and reread the story of Adam and Eve and how sin came into the world. Later that week, Jessica was ill and had to stay home from school. Feeling miserable, she told me, "If only Adam and Eve hadn't eaten the fruit, I wouldn't be sick." Before I could answer, she quickly added, "But, of course, if they hadn't eaten it, we'd be sitting here naked!"

—Sarah Ames
KOBE, JAPAN

"Pastor, your ten o'clock counseling session and last Sunday's sermon illustration are here!"

Lost in the Service

One Sunday morning, Pastor McGhee noticed that little Alex was staring up at the large plaque that hung in the foyer of the church. The seven-year-old had been staring at the plaque for some time, so the pastor walked up, stood beside the boy, and said quietly, "Good morning, Alex."

"Good morning," replied the boy. Still focused on the plaque, he asked, "Pastor McGhee, what is this?"

"Well, son, these are all the people who have died in the service," replied the pastor.

Soberly they stood together, staring at the long list of names.

Little Alex's voice barely broke the silence when he asked quietly, "Which one—the 9:00 or the 10:30 service?"

—Krista VanGorp

SAVANNAH, GEORGIA

Pastor Brackerman secretly wishes that certain folks would leave analogy-making to the professionals.

Big Ed's Hearing

Big Ed goes to the revival and listens to the preacher. After a while the preacher asks anyone with needs to come forward to be prayed over. Big Ed gets in line. When it's his turn, the preacher says, "Big Ed, what do you want me to pray about?"

Big Ed says, "Preacher, I need you to pray for my hearing."

So the preacher puts one finger in Big Ed's ear and the other hand on top of his head and shouts, hollers, and prays awhile.

After a few minutes, he removes his hands and says, "Big Ed, how's your hearing now?"

Big Ed says, "I don't know, preacher. It's not until next Wednesday at the Dupage County Courthouse."

—Marshall Shelley
GLEN ELLYN, ILLINOIS

Always Finding Fault

An elderly man lay in a hospital with his wife of fifty-five years sitting at his bedside. "Is that you, Ethel, at my side again?" he whispered.

"Yes, dear," she answered.

He softly said to her, "Remember years ago when I was in the Veteran's Hospital? You were with me then. You were with me when we lost everything in a fire. And, Ethel, when we were poor, you stuck with me then too."

The man sighed and said, "I tell you, Ethel. You are bad luck."

FROM PREACHINGTODAY.COM

Quick Thinking

To start a discussion on core values, our youth pastor asked the teenagers: "What would you do if your doctor told you that you had only twenty-four hours to live?"

The teens mentioned being with friends and family, and the discussion seemed headed in the right direction. But it came undone when Jason, our thirteen-year-old, said, "I'd get a second opinion."

—Donna Spratt
MELFORT, SASKATCHEWAN

Find Spiritual Formation Tools at
ChristianBibleStudies.com

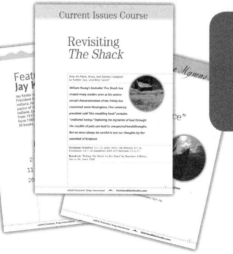